Word of the Day

Bit by Bit

Heather McDonald

Primary Concepts®

Cover illustration: Happy Families, Samuel, age 7, Little Fish Art, Edison, NJ
©River of Words

Editor: Ann Roper
Design: Candace Wesen

©2007 Primary Concepts
P.O. Box 10043
Berkeley, CA 94709

All rights reserved.
Printed in the U.S.A.

No part of this book may be reproduced, stored in a retrieval system or transmitted
in any form or by any means, electronic, mechanical, photocopying, recording, or otherwise,
without the prior written permission of the publisher.

ISBN 978-1-893791-99-2

Contents

Word of the Day . . .iv	undercover 15	overdue 30	irreparable 45
cheerful 1	population 16	postpone 31	marina 46
miniature 2	exterior 17	preview 32	microscope 47
captain 3	vision 18	construction 33	multicolored 48
aquarium 4	automatic 19	subway 34	symphony 49
duet 5	conference 20	tripod 35	portable 50
careless 6	inhale 21	astronomy 36	request 51
impossible 7	unable 22	audio 37	supervise 52
midnight 8	bilingual 23	biography 38	telescope 53
misunderstand 9	century 24	flexible 39	territory 54
washable 10	dishonesty 25	thermostat 40	transfer 55
octopus 11	magnificent 26	contrary 41	unicorn 56
pedestrian 12	memorable 27	stethoscope 42	Index 57, 58
selfish 13	millionaire 28	cyclone 43	
musician 14	nonstop 29	interrupt 44	

Word of the Day: Bit by Bit

©Primary Concepts

Word of the Day

Word of the Day books are designed to help young children develop an appreciation for interesting vocabulary words. The goal is to set a foundation for a lifelong love of words. They are also intended to introduce young children to a way of building their oral vocabularies one word at a time, a routine that will serve them well for the rest of their lives.

Setting this foundation for word learning in the primary grades is important, because as early as 4th grade, children's reading comprehension skills suffer from poor word knowledge. While many of today's children are developing oral vocabularies at a prodigious rate, others are falling behind.

Bit by Bit

Word of the Day: Bit by Bit introduces children to common word parts that can help them know the meanings of words. These word parts can be prefixes, suffixes, or root words. Like its parent book, *Word of the Day,* each lesson is comprised of short oral activities. You may wish to weave lessons from this book with words from the parent book. You can pick and choose lessons, or start on the first page and proceed through to the final word in this book.

Children who are familiar with *Word of the Day* will recognize the Wordly family. Each lesson is introduced with a story about the Wordly family in which the word of the day comes into play. Get started with the lesson by reading the story. Write the word of the day on the board. Highlight the focus word part and tell the children what the word part typically means. Then summarize the meaning of the word of the day in words the children can understand.

Next, record the other words listed that contain the same word part. Highlight the word part in each word. Use the questions in the Talk About It section to get children started using the words in conversation.

Making It Meaningful

Suggestions are provided for active ways for children to build meaning for words that contain the word part. Sometimes you might have children draw a picture, act out a part, find examples of a word in the classroom, and so on. These short activities are intended to help children remember the word and its word part in a context they understand.

After you have introduced the word, challenge the children to use words with the new word part over the next week or so, either in school or after school. Write each new word with its highlighted word part on a 3" × 5" card. Keep a jar in your classroom and put each new card in it before you move on to the next word. Periodically, pull out a word card and see if the children can remember what the word and its word part mean. Ask them to use the word in a sentence.

cheerful ful (full)

Word Story

The Wordlys are an imaginary American family. There are many children in the family, and they all seem to enjoy each other. They are a cheerful bunch, interested in many things, including, of course, words.

If you are *cheerful*, you are happy. You are full of cheer.

In Other Words

fearful   thoughtful   careful   painful

Talk About It
- Who in our class would you call cheerful? Why?
- What are you fearful of?
- Do you know anyone who is especially thoughtful?

Act It Out

Pick a word that ends with the word part *ful*, such as *cheerful, fearful, careful, thoughtful, painful*. Without speaking, show us how you would look if you are feeling that way, and we will try to guess your word.

©Primary Concepts

2

miniature mini (small)

Word Story

The youngest Wordly girl was especially pleased with one of her birthday gifts this year. It was a miniature tea set. Each cup holds just a sip of tea, and she can hold the pot in the palm of her hand. She uses the set to host tea parties for her dolls. It's the perfect size.

Something that's *miniature* is very small.

In Other Words

minivan   minimize

Talk About It

- Do you have anything that's a miniature copy of something that's actually larger?
- Why is a minivan called a *mini* van?
- How could you minimize the damage if your dog dug up someone's flowers?

Act It Out

Pretend you are making things for a family of miniature people. You need to use common objects easily found around the house. For example, a thimble could be a bucket, and a paintbrush a mop. Let's make a list of objects and what they could be used for.

©Primary Concepts

captain cap (head)

Word Story

The oldest Wordly boy was chosen as captain of his basketball team. He's a good leader, and sets a good example for the other players.

A *captain* is the head, or leader, of a group.

In Other Words

capital   capitol   cap

Talk About It

- Have you ever been the captain of a group or team?
- What's the capital of our state? Have you ever been to the capitol building?
- When do we use capital letters?
- Where does a baseball cap go? Where does a bottle cap go?

Write It

Write the alphabet in capital letters. Make them look strong and bold as if they are the leaders, or heads, of their words.

©Primary Concepts

aquarium aqua (water)

Word Story

The most interesting feature of the Wordlys' living room is their huge aquarium. It is filled with all sorts of brilliantly colored fish that could be found in the ocean.

An *aquarium* is a tank filled with water for fish to live in.

In Other Words

aquatic   aqua

Talk About It

- ✪ Have you ever been to an aquarium? Tell about a few creatures you saw there.
- ✪ Let's make a list of aquatic animals.
- ✪ What color is aqua? How do you think it got its name?

Find It

Find something in the room that is aqua in color.

©Primary Concepts

duet du (two)

Word Story

At her band concert, one of the Wordly girls is playing a duet with her friend. The song is a pretty piece for two flutes, with one player echoing the other. It sounds like two little birds calling to each other playfully.

A *duet* is a piece performed by two musicians or singers.

In Other Words

duplicate   duo   duplex

Talk About It

- Have you ever played or sung a duet with someone?
- If you lived in a duplex, who would you like to live on its other side?
- If you could duplicate one experience you've had in your life to live over again, what would it be?

Do It

Get a partner and think of a song to sing together. Practice a few times, then perform your duet for the class. What do you call your duo?

©Primary Concepts

careless less (without)

6

Word Story

The Wordly children don't always take good care of their toys. They often leave them outside. "It could rain tonight. Or someone might take your things if you don't bring them inside," Mr. Wordly always tells them. "Don't be so careless."

If you are *careless*, you don't take care of something—you are without care.

In Other Words

painless   endless   cloudless   fearless

Talk About It

- ✪ Are you careless or careful with your toys?
- ✪ What does a cloudless day look like?
- ✪ What is the opposite of fearless? painless?
- ✪ Describe a day that seemed endless to you.

Picture It

Choose one of these pairs of opposites: careful/careless, fearful/fearless, painful/painless. Draw a picture to illustrate both words.

©Primary Concepts

impossible im (not)

Word Story

After the Wordlys' car got dented, their mechanic fixed it so that it's impossible to tell there was ever any damage. There's no sign of a dent or a scratch at all.

When we say something is *impossible*, we mean that it is not possible.

In Other Words

impolite   imperfect   immature

Talk About It
- List some events that are impossible.
- What are some polite behaviors and their impolite opposites?
- What is the opposite of mature? perfect?

Write It

Pretend you were late for school. Make up one excuse that would be possible for your teacher to believe, and one that would be impossible to believe.

©Primary Concepts

midnight mid (middle)

8

Word Story

On New Year's Eve, the Wordlys like to stay up until midnight. They usually play board games and watch a family movie together. Then they toot horns and pull apart "poppers," filling the room with paper streamers.

Midnight is 12:00 A.M.

In Other Words

midday   midair   midsummer   midsize   midway

Talk About It

- ✪ What time is it at midday? What are you usually doing in the middle of the day?
- ✪ Name some things that you might see in midair.
- ✪ When is midsummer? What are you usually doing at that time?
- ✪ Do you know anyone with a midsize car?

Picture It

Draw a square on the left side of a paper. Now draw a circle on the right side. Draw a triangle midway between the square and the circle.

©Primary Concepts

misunderstand mis (wrong)

Word Story
Mr. Wordly misunderstood what his daughter was saying. He thought she said he was a bore, when she really said she needed him to take her to the store!

If you *misunderstand* something, you understand it or hear it the wrong way.

In Other Words
mistake   misspell   misbehave   misplace

Talk About It
- What mistake did Mr. Wordly make?
- Do you ever misbehave?
- Have you ever misplaced something?
- Can you spell the word *misspell?* If you don't spell it correctly, what have you done?

Write It
Write a spelling mistake. Then we'll figure out what you did wrong.

©Primary Concepts

10

washable able (can)

Word Story

When the little Wordly girl got her new tennis shoes muddy by mistake, she cried and cried. "Don't worry," her mother told her. "Those are washable. We'll have them clean in no time!"

If something is *washable*, it can be washed.

In Other Words

changeable   readable   rechargeable   comfortable

Talk About It

- Can you think of anything that is not washable?
- Name some things that are rechargeable.
- What is the opposite of comfortable?

Write It

Write a sentence in your most readable handwriting. Now write that same sentence in printing that is hard to read.

©Primary Concepts

octopus oct (eight)

Word Story

During winter break, the Wordlys visited an aquarium where they saw a giant octopus. The octopus was slowly moving in the aquarium tank. It was fascinating to watch.

An *octopus* is a sea animal with eight arms.

In Other Words

octagon   October

Talk About It

- Have you ever seen an octopus? How are eight arms helpful to the octopus?
- A pentagon has five sides. How many sides do you think an octagon has?
- In ancient times, October was the eighth month of the year. Now it is the tenth month. What are some things that happen in October?

Picture It

Draw an Octoman. It should have eight of something—eight eyes or legs, for example.

©Primary Concepts

pedestrian ped (foot)

12

Word Story

The oldest Wordly boy is learning how to drive. It makes Mr. and Mrs. Wordly nervous to ride in the car with him. They are always saying things like, "Do you see the stop sign?" "Slow down!" "Watch out for that pedestrian!"

A *pedestrian* is someone who walks on foot.

In Other Words

pedal   pedometer   pedicure

Talk About It

- ✪ Where do you see pedestrians?
- ✪ What is a pedal? How does it relate to *ped*, meaning *foot?*
- ✪ What does a pedometer measure? Have you ever used one?
- ✪ Has anyone here ever had a manicure or a pedicure?

Act It Out   *Materials: green and red paper*

Be pedestrians. When I show the green paper, you can walk. If I'm holding up the red paper, you need to stop and wait for the green.

©Primary Concepts

selfish self (oneself)

Word Story
Sometimes the youngest Wordly boy thinks his sister is selfish when she wants their mother to read to her privately. She just wants a bit of time with her mother, but he thinks he should be included.

A person who is *selfish* thinks only about themselves and what they want.

In Other Words
self-confidence   self-control   self-service

Talk About It
- Do you think the Wordly girl is selfish for wanting alone-time with her mom?
- What is self-service gasoline?
- Who do you know who has lots of self-confidence?
- Have you ever lost your self-control? What happened?

Act It Out
Work with a partner. One of you acts selfish. The other acts unselfish. Have a conversation about who should be first to do something you both want to do.

©Primary Concepts

musician ician (one who)

Word Story

The Wordlys' friend is a professional musician. Her job is to practice and perform with her rock band, Crazy Cactus. They have a strange name, but they're all great musicians!

A *musician* is a person who plays music.

In Other Words

politician   magician   physician

Talk About It

- What is the job of a politician? a magician? a physician?
- Can you name any famous politicians? how about musicians?
- Have you ever seen a magician perform? What kinds of tricks did they do?
- There are many types of physicians. Is your physician a pediatrician?

Write It

Do you have a favorite musician? Write about that person—what instrument he or she plays, what type of music the musician performs.

©Primary Concepts

undercover under (under)

Word Story
When Mrs. Wordly was young, she dreamed of being an undercover spy. She would appear to all her friends and neighbors to be an ordinary person, but all the while she would be carrying out top-secret spy missions.

Someone who is *undercover* is doing something secretly while trying to appear normal.

In Other Words
underground   underwear   underdog

Talk About It
- Name some things we might find underground.
- Why do we call underwear *underwear*? What is it under?
- What do we mean when we say a team is the *underdog* in a game? Do you usually root for the underdog?

Act It Out
Pretend you are a spy on an undercover mission. Move around the classroom as if you were a spy.

©Primary Concepts

population pop (people)

Word Story

The population of the Wordlys' small town is 9,875. The largest nearby city has a population of 97,000. It's almost ten times bigger than the Wordlys' town.

Population is the number of all the people who live in a place.

In Other Words

populate   popular

Talk About It

- Do you think the population of our city is getting bigger or smaller each year?
- How does the meaning of the word *popular* relate to people?
- Have you ever heard of pop music? What do you think *pop* is short for?

Act It Out

After school, see if you can find out the population of our city. How might you be able to find out? What resources could you use?

©Primary Concepts

exterior ex (out)

Word Story

The Wordlys are painting the exterior of their house. Everyone in the family has a favorite color they want it to be. One of the Wordly boys thinks it should be painted pumpkin orange. Finally, Mrs. Wordly decided it will be a cheerful yellow color.

The *exterior* of something is the outside of it.

In Other Words

exit   expedition   exhale

Talk About It
- Why is it important to know where a building's exits are?
- If you could set out on an expedition, where would you go?

Do It

Try exhaling in these different ways:
- Exhale loudly, in a puff of air.
- Exhale as slowly as you can.
- Exhale five quick puffs of air.

©Primary Concepts

vision vis (sight)

18

Word Story

All of the Wordly children have excellent vision. None of them needs glasses so far. Mr. Wordly also has great vision, and Mrs. Wordly just recently got glasses for reading.

Vision is the ability to see.

In Other Words

visual   visible   visit

Talk About It

- When you read or listen to a story, do you form visual images in your mind?
- Name some things that are visible. What are some things that are invisible (*not* visible)?
- Who is your favorite person to go see, or visit?

Act It Out

What might it be like to have no vision? Work with a partner and take turns helping each other move around the classroom as if one of you has lost vision.

©Primary Concepts

automatic auto (self)

Word Story
The Wordlys' new van has automatic doors. At first Mr. Wordly didn't tell the children about it. Instead, he pretended he was magic and could close the doors with a simple snap of his fingers. The children were astounded every time!

Something that is *automatic* works by itself.

In Other Words
automobile   autograph

Talk About It
- Can you think of things that you have or use that work automatically?
- Why do you think we rarely hear the term *automobile* any more?
- Whose autograph would you like to get? Why?

Picture It
Imagine you could invent something automatic. What would it be? Draw a picture of your new invention.

©Primary Concepts

conference con (together, with)

20

Word Story

The Wordly children always look forward to the day Mrs. Wordly comes back from a conference. They miss her when she is gone, and she always brings home something interesting for each of her children. One time she brought home an autographed copy of a book from one of the children's favorite authors.

A *conference* is when people meet together about a certain topic.

In Other Words

connect   conversation   con

Talk About It

✪ List some things that are connected, or put together.
✪ Name a person you like to have conversations with. What do you talk about?
✪ A *con* is a point against a certain decision. What are the pros and cons of getting a pet?

Act It Out

Work together with a partner, pretending you are having a parent-teacher conference. One of you is a parent, one the teacher. Then switch roles.

©Primary Concepts

inhale in (in)

Word Story
Mrs. Wordly is funny. She loves to inhale the rich smell of fresh coffee, but she doesn't like to drink it. She says she's never liked the taste of coffee—just the smell.

To *inhale* is to breathe in.

In Other Words
inside   interior   income   infection

Talk About It
- Which two of the In Other Words words mean the same thing?
- Have you heard of an interior decorator? What do you think that person's job is?
- What is the opposite of inside? What is the opposite of interior?
- Do you have any income of your own? How do you make money?
- What comes in when you have an infection?

Do It
Inhale deeply. Then exhale all of the air you inhaled.

©Primary Concepts

22

unable un (not)

Word Story

One Wordly daughter was disappointed because she was unable to go swimming with her friends. She couldn't do it because she was just getting over an ear infection and her doctor said she shouldn't swim for a week.

If you are *unable* to do something, you are not able to do it.

In Other Words

uncomfortable   unbutton   uncertain

Talk About It

- ✪ Tell about a time when you were uncomfortable. In what way were you not feeling comfortable?
- ✪ Who is wearing something that needs to be unbuttoned? untied? unzipped?
- ✪ What other words can you think of that mean the same thing as uncertain?

Find Out

Look in a dictionary. How many words do you think begin with *un*?

©Primary Concepts

bilingual bi (two)

Word Story

Mr. Wordly is bilingual. He speaks both Spanish and English. He frequently speaks both languages to his children so that they can be bilingual, too.

Someone who is *bilingual* speaks two languages.

In Other Words

bicycle   binoculars   bifocals

Talk About It

- Are you bilingual? Which languages do you speak?
- What do binoculars help you do?
- A bicycle has two wheels. What is a cycle with three wheels called? one wheel?
- Do you know anyone who wears bifocals? What are there two of in this type of glasses?

Make a List

Let's make a list of words we know from other languages.

©Primary Concepts

24

century cent (hundred)

Word Story

A beautiful tree near the Wordlys' house is over a century old. They have seen a picture of their area taken 100 years ago, and the tree is actually in that picture!

A *century* is a period of one hundred years.

In Other Words

cent   centimeter   centipede

Talk About It

○ Why is a penny called a cent? What does its name have to do with the number one hundred?

○ Centimeters are very small. Can you guess how many centimeters are in a meter?

○ Show with your fingers about how big a centimeter is.

○ Do you think a centipede really has one hundred legs?

Picture It

Draw a picture of a centipede — a bug with many pairs of legs.

©Primary Concepts

dishonesty dis (not or without)

Word Story
If there's one thing Mrs. Wordly won't stand for, it's dishonesty. She expects her children to tell her the truth, no matter what. She tells them that because they are so trustworthy, she can let them have more responsibility and independence.

Dishonesty means lying or not telling the whole truth.

In Other Words
disagree   discover   disbelief

Talk About It
- Name one thing that you have disagreed with someone about recently.
- Are there any rules here at school that you disagree with?
- What does the word *discover* have to do with the word part meaning *not* or *without*?

Act It Out
Pretend someone just told you something unbelievable, and you are reacting in disbelief. How would your face look?

©Primary Concepts

magnificent mag (great)

Word Story

One of the Wordly children found a tiny insect outside. He used the magnifying glass he got as a birthday gift to look closely at the insect. The insect had a magnificent pattern of yellow and orange on its body.

Something that is *magnificent* is impressive, beautiful, or great in some way.

In Other Words

magnify   magnitude

Talk About It

- ✪ Have you ever used a magnifying glass? What for?
- ✪ What's the most magnificent scenery you've ever seen? Describe it.
- ✪ The magnitude of an earthquake is its size. How do you think a small magnitude earthquake would feel? a big one?

Write It

Write your name regular-size. Now write it again, as if it's under a magnifying glass.

©Primary Concepts

memorable mem (memory)

Word Story
A memorable event in the Wordly family was the time their cat Petunia disappeared. Apparently Petunia had gotten locked in the neighbor's garage while they were away. All the Wordlys were glad when Petunia came back.

Something is *memorable* if you won't easily forget it. You will probably remember it forever.

In Other Words
remember   memory   memorize   memorial

Talk About It
- What is a memorable event in your life?
- Do you have a good memory for facts? instructions? things you've read?
- What kinds of things are important to memorize? (address, phone number, math facts…)
- Why do Americans observe Memorial Day?

Picture It
Draw a picture to show a memorable event in your life.

©Primary Concepts

millionaire mil (thousand)

28

Word Story

One evening at the dinner table, the Wordly family talked about what they would do if they were millionaires. Everyone had their own ideas about what they would do with a lot of money. The smallest Wordly had the best idea. She thought it would be good to use the money to help homeless people.

A *millionaire* has money or property worth over a million dollars.

In Other Words

millennium   millipede   million

Talk About It

- ✪ Had you been born when we celebrated the millennium?
- ✪ Have you ever seen a millipede? Do you think it really has a thousand legs?
- ✪ Where could you find a million of something?

Picture It

Draw a picture of what you would do if you were a millionaire.

©Primary Concepts

nonstop non (not)

Word Story

A little Wordly boy came home from school and began talking nonstop. He was telling about something that happened that day, but he was so excited his story didn't make any sense at all.

When you do something *nonstop*, you do not stop.

In Other Words

nonsense   nonfiction   nonviolent

Talk About It

- What is a nonstop train?
- Which do you like to read better — fiction or nonfiction? What's the difference?
- Name some movies or video games that are nonviolent.

Write It

Make up a nonsense rhyme. For instance, you might write:

> Once a mouse
> Leapt over a house!

©Primary Concepts

overdue over (more or above)

30

Word Story

Mrs. Wordly was horrified when she got a call from the library saying that the Wordlys had 23 overdue library books! Luckily, they were only one day past the due date, and she returned them that very afternoon.

If something is *overdue*, it's gone over the due date.

In Other Words

overpriced overdo overpass

Talk About It

✪ Have you ever wanted to buy something, but your mom said it was overpriced?

✪ What does it mean when someone says, "Don't overdo it."

✪ Why do some roads have overpasses? What is an overpass for?

Act It Out

Pretend you are Wordly kids and your mom told you to be polite at a party. Act out a scene with your partner(s) to show how you might go overboard with good manners.

©Primary Concepts

postpone   post (after)

Word Story
When the Wordlys all came down with the flu last week, they had to postpone their camping trip that was scheduled for that weekend. They knew they wouldn't have the energy to enjoy the experience.

When you *postpone* something, you reschedule it for after the original date.

In Other Words
postscript (P.S.)   posttest

Talk About It
- Has your family ever needed to postpone an event? What happened to make you change the date?
- Have you ever written a P.S. in a letter? How about a P.P.S.? What would P.P.S. mean?
- What is the opposite of a pretest? What is the difference between a pretest and a posttest?

Write It
Write a short note to a friend and include a postscript.

©Primary Concepts

preview pre (before)

Word Story

The Wordlys always make sure to get to the movies early so they can watch the previews. They want to see which upcoming movies look good, and which ones they should skip.

A *preview* is a short sample of a movie shown before the actual movie is out in theaters.

In Other Words

preschool   prehistoric   preteen   previous

Talk About It

- How many of you went to preschool?
- Name some creatures that lived in prehistoric times.
- Do you know any big kids who are preteens? What ages are considered preteen?
- I am your current teacher. Which teachers have you had in previous years?

Act It Out

Work with a partner to act out a preview of a book you've both read. The preview will help other children in our class decide if they are interested in reading that book.

©Primary Concepts

construction struct (build)

Word Story
There is a lot of construction going on at the house next to the Wordlys. The neighbors decided they needed more room in their house, so they are building a second story addition. Upstairs will be two new bedrooms, a bathroom, and an office space.

Construction is the work of building buildings, or structures.

In Other Words
construct   structure   instruct

Talk About It
- Do you like to construct things out of building blocks or plastic building sets? What do you like to make?
- What types of structures do we have in our town? Let's list as many types as we can.
- What are teachers *building* when they in*struct* students?

Picture It
Draw a picture of the structure you live in.

©Primary Concepts

subway sub (under)

Word Story

Mr. Wordly didn't want to drive the car to the baseball game. It was too far to walk, so the family decided to take the subway.

A *subway* is an underground train.

In Other Words

submarine   subtitle

Talk About It

✪ Have you ever been on a subway? Tell us about it.
✪ Do you remember what marine means? Where might you find a submarine?
✪ Where would you see a subtitle?

Find It

Find a book in our classroom or in the library that has a subtitle. How does the title compare to the subtitle in terms of size? Copy the title in big, bold letters. Then, under the title write the subtitle in much smaller letters.

©Primary Concepts

tripod tri (three)

Word Story
Mr. Wordly wanted to take a picture of the whole family and all of their pets. He put his camera on a tripod so he didn't have to hold it. Then he ran to get into the photo before the timer went off. With each photo there was a problem. Someone was making a silly face or someone was hidden behind someone else. Finally Mr. Wordly got a picture he was happy with.

A *tripod* is a three-legged stand.

In Other Words
tricycle   triangle   triplet

Talk About It
- How is the word part *tri* like the word *three*?
- What are there three of in a tricycle? a triangle? triplets?

Picture It
Draw a picture of a Tri-Monster. Give your monster three eyes, three ears, three arms, three legs, and so on.

©Primary Concepts

astronomy astro, aster (star)

36

Word Story

One of the Wordly girls is fascinated by astronomy. She can name planets and stars in the night sky. She wants to be an astronomer when she grows up.

When you study *astronomy*, you study the stars, planets, and space.

In Other Words

astronaut   asterisk

Talk About It

- Do you think astronaut is a good name for astronauts? Why or why not?
- Do you know anyone who is especially interested in astronomy?

Find It

An asterisk is a mark (*) used to tell readers to look somewhere else on a page to get more information. Look for an asterisk on a computer keyboard or in a book. What does it look like?

©Primary Concepts

audio   aud (hear)

Word Story
When Mr. Wordly hooked up the family's new television, the audio wasn't working. They couldn't hear the sound at all. Something was wrong. Maybe he forgot to connect one of the cables.

Audio is the sound signal on an electronic device.

In Other Words
audible   auditorium   audience   audition

Talk About It
- What do the words *auditorium, audience,* and *audition* have to do with hearing or sound?
- Name some sounds that are audible right now in the classroom.

Do It
Let's take turns with an audio guessing game. We'll close our eyes while one classmate makes a noise (tongue clucking, finger snapping, zipping a zipper, tapping a pencil, etc.). Raise your hand when you have a guess about what's making the sound.

©Primary Concepts

biography bio (life)

38

Word Story

One of the Wordly girls is very interested in Helen Keller and just read a fascinating biography of her life. She also recently read Helen's autobiography *The Story of My Life* in which Helen wrote her life story.

A *biography* is the story of someone's life.

In Other Words

biology   biologist

Talk About It

- ✪ Have you ever read a biography? Who was it about?
- ✪ If you were a biologist, what plants or animals would you choose to study?

Write It

Pretend you are going to write a biography of your best friend. Write the first paragraph. Make it lively and entertaining. It should capture the most important part of your friend's personality.

©Primary Concepts

flexible flex (bend)

Word Story
The Wordlys' little neighbor is extremely flexible. She can lie on her stomach and then bend her toes toward her ears, making the shape of an O!

Something that is *flexible* is easily bendable.

In Other Words
flex   reflex   inflexible

Talk About It
- Name some things that are flexible.
- What is the opposite of flexible? Name some things that are inflexible.
- Are your reflexes fast or slow? What does it mean to flex your muscles?

Do It
Try these exercises to test your flexibility:

Sit down and bend your head toward your toes gently.
Stand up with your arms over your head and bend gently to one side.
Stand up and bend down to touch your toes.

©Primary Concepts

thermostat therm (heat)

40

Word Story

Just as the cold weather of winter came, the Wordlys' thermostat broke. They couldn't control the heater, so it was much too cold inside the house. They will need to get this fixed right away if they don't want to turn into popsicles!

A *thermostat* controls the heating system in a building.

In Other Words

thermometer   thermos   thermal

Talk About It

✪ What does a thermometer measure?

✪ Do any of you have a thermos in your lunchbox? What is a thermos for?

✪ In some cold climates, people wear thermal (long) underwear. Why?

Picture It

Draw two pictures of an outdoor thermometer. Label each from zero to one hundred by tens (10, 20, 30…). On one thermometer, color the bar to show a summer day temperature. On the other, color the bar to show a winter day temperature.

©Primary Concepts

contrary contra (against)

Word Story
That middle Wordly girl is so contrary! It seems she always disagrees with everyone. When her friends are trying to decide what to do, she votes against what the others want.

A person who is *contrary* goes against the opinions or wishes of others.

In Other Words
contradict   contrast

Talk About It
- Do you ever act contrary? Do you usually have good reasons for going against the popular opinion?
- When you contrast two things, you compare one thing against another, looking for differences. How might you contrast two things such as a football and a basketball?

Picture It
Draw a picture that shows the contrasts between you and your best friend.

©Primary Concepts

42 stethoscope scope (instrument for viewing)

Word Story

The Wordlys' family doctor always lets the Wordly children use her stethoscope to listen to their own heartbeats. The children look forward to their visits to the doctor.

A *stethoscope* is an instrument for listening to sounds in a person's heart or lungs.

In Other Words

microscope   telescope   periscope

Talk About It

- Where might you find a microscope? a telescope? a periscope?
- Who might use each of those types of scope?

Picture It

Imagine you are looking at a butterfly wing through a microscope. Draw a picture of what it might look like.

©Primary Concepts

cyclone cycle (circle)

Word Story

One day Mrs. Wordly exclaimed, "It looks like a cyclone has hit the house." Everyone looked around and had to agree. It looked as if a storm had picked up everyone's toys and tossed them every which way. It was time for a big clean up.

A *cyclone* is a storm with very high winds that swirl around in a circle.

In Other Words

bicycle   recycle

Talk About It

- Do you recycle? What kinds of things do you recycle? How is recycling like a circle?
- What has a circle shape on a bicycle?

Picture It   *Materials: circle shapes, drawing materials*

The seasons are cyclical (like a circle). To show this, fold a circle shape in half, and then in half again to form four areas. In each area, picture a season of the year. Start with spring, then summer, fall, and winter.

©Primary Concepts

interrupt inter (between)

Word Story

A younger Wordly girl needs to break one of her habits. She tends to interrupt people a lot. She has a hard time holding her thoughts or questions until there's an appropriate break in the conversation. At school, she forgets to raise her hand and just pipes right up.

When you *interrupt*, you break the flow of action or conversation between others.

In Other Words

international   intervene   intercept

Talk About It

- ✪ Do you have a habit of interrupting? How could someone break that habit?
- ✪ Have you ever had an argument with someone that required an adult to intervene?
- ✪ Have you ever traveled internationally? Where did you go?
- ✪ What does it mean when a football player intercepts a pass?

Act It Out

Make up a short skit with a partner or two. The skit should show some sort of interruption.

©Primary Concepts

irreparable ir (not)

Word Story

None of the Wordly children thought much about the family's water heater until one day it broke down. Everyone had to use cold water. Taking a shower was like washing in ice. The water heater repairman examined the water heater and said it was irreparable. It couldn't be fixed and they would just need to get a new one.

If something is *irreparable*, it cannot be repaired.

In Other Words

irresponsible   irregular   irreplaceable

Talk About It

- Have you ever had anything that got broken and was irreparable? What happened?
- Are you ever irresponsible? What do you do that's not very responsible?
- What's the last irregular, or out of the ordinary, thing that's happened to you?

Picture It

Draw a picture and write a description of one item that would be irreplaceable if you lost it or it got destroyed somehow. Tell why it's so important to you, and where you got it.

©Primary Concepts

marina mar (sea)

Word Story

On vacation, the Wordly family decided to visit a marina. At the marina, they saw lots of different kinds of boats. It made them think they might want to own a boat some day.

A *marina* is a place for mooring boats.

In Other Words

marine   submarine   aquamarine

Talk About It

- Have any of you been to a marina?
- Does anyone know someone who is in the Marines? Where do Marines serve our country?
- *Sub* means *under*. What does a submarine go under?
- What color is aquamarine?

Picture It   *Materials: crayons, watercolors, brushes*

Draw a picture of marine life with crayons. Then paint over your sea creatures with an aquamarine watercolor wash.

©Primary Concepts

microscope micro (small)

Word Story

At school, the oldest Wordly boy uses a microscope to look at the body structures of very small things like ants and gnats. The microscope makes the bugs look bigger, so the students can see their details better.

A *microscope* magnifies small objects so they are easier to see.

In Other Words

microwave   microscopic

Talk About It

- What kinds of things are microscopic?
- What does the *micro* (small) refer to in *microwave*?

Make a List

Let's use our imaginations to make up some words that begin with *micro*.

> Example: micromommy—a Chihuahua with puppies
> microsnack—an ant's snack

©Primary Concepts

multicolored multi (many)

48

Word Story

For her birthday, the Wordly children all pitched in and bought their mother a beautiful, multicolored scarf. It has all the shades she loves the best—sage, peach, teal, and sepia. It matches lots of her work clothes.

Something that has many colors is called *multicolored*.

In Other Words

multicultural   multimedia   multiply   multimillionaire

Talk About It

✪ Would you say our school has a multicultural population? Explain.

✪ How could our class make a multimedia presentation?

✪ What do you do when you multiply? How does the word *multiply* relate to the word meaning of *multi-,* meaning *many?*

✪ Can you name any famous people who are probably multimillionaires?

Picture It

Draw a picture of something that is multicolored.

©Primary Concepts

symphony phone (sound)

Word Story

One Wordly neighbor is a cello player in a symphony orchestra. Once the family went to the symphony to hear her orchestra perform — what a great sound they made all together!

A *symphony* orchestra is a large musical group that includes string, wind, and percussion instruments.

In Other Words

telephone   phonetic   microphone

Talk About It

- *Sym-* means *together*. What is the literal meaning of the word *symphony*?
- How might you spell the word *phone* phonetically?
- When might you hear someone speaking over a microphone?

Act It Out

Pretend that you are playing an instrument in the symphony. We'll try to guess what instrument you are playing.

©Primary Concepts

portable port (carry)

Word Story

When the Wordly children were small, the family kept a portable crib in the back of their van. Any time they were out visiting and the baby needed to take a nap, they would just unfold the crib and set it up.

If something is *portable*, it is easily carried from one place to another.

In Other Words

transportation　　　porter　　　support

Talk About It

- ✪ Do you have any portable items that your family uses?
- ✪ How are you transported to school each day?
- ✪ Has a porter ever carried your luggage at an airport?

Picture It

Make an advertisement for something that is portable. Draw a picture of it. Write the word portable on your ad.

©Primary Concepts

request ques or quer (ask)

Word Story

The oldest Wordly girl has a request. She wants to be allowed to stay out late Friday night. She is usually expected home by 10:00, but she wants to go to a movie with her friends that doesn't end until 10:20. She hopes her parents will grant her request.

Request means to ask for something.

In Other Words

question   query   questionnaire

Talk About It

- Do you have any requests for changes at school?
- Have you ever filled out a questionnaire or a survey? What was it about?

Write It

Write to your teacher with a request.

©Primary Concepts

supervise super (above or beyond)

52

Word Story

Mrs. Wordly was asked to help supervise the playground at school on a day the teachers were having a special lunch. She needed to keep an eye on the children and make sure everyone followed the rules. It was a treat for the Wordly children to have their mom at school.

If you *supervise* a group of people, you watch over them. You are in charge.

In Other Words

superhero   supermarket   superdome

Talk About It

✪ What *super*heroes do you know of? What are their superior powers?

✪ What is *super* about a supermarket?

✪ Does anyone know where the Superdome is? Why do you think it is called that?

Picture It

If you were a superhero, what would your name be and what special powers would you have? Draw a picture of yourself in your superhero costume.

©Primary Concepts

telescope tele (far away)

Word Story
One of the Wordly girls is interested in the night sky. She is saving her money to get a telescope so that she can see the stars and planets close up.

A *telescope* is an instrument that makes faraway objects appear larger and closer.

In Other Words
telephone   television   telephoto

Talk About It
- Have you ever used a telescope to see things in the night sky?
- What is *far away* when you use a telescope? a telephone? a television?
- What's the farthest distance your family usually calls on the telephone?
- What does a camera's telephoto lens help you do?

Find Out
Do you know your telephone number? How about your mom's and dad's cell phone numbers? Write them down. If you don't know them, find out tonight at home.

©Primary Concepts

territory terr (earth)

Word Story

The Wordlys' kitten is getting bigger. She is learning how to be outdoors and come home when called with Mrs. Wordly's special whistle sound. Her territory is slowly growing, as one by one she explores the neighbors' yards.

Territory is an area of land.

In Other Words

terrarium   terrain   terrier

Talk About It

- ✪ What's the difference between a terrarium and an aquarium?
- ✪ What type of terrain do you like to hike on — flat, hilly, steep, rocky …?
- ✪ Terriers are dogs that were originally used for chasing small animals from their holes or dens. How does this relate to the word meaning of *terr* (earth)?

Picture It

Draw a picture of your favorite type of terrain. You might love mountains or rolling hills, shady valleys or flat plains.

©Primary Concepts

transfer trans (change or across)

Word Story
Last year, the oldest Wordly boy transferred from one school to another. He was really interested in math and science, so he changed to a school that focused on those subjects.

When you *transfer*, you change from one thing to another.

In Other Words
transport   translate   transmit   transplant

Talk About It
- Foods are often transported from where they are grown to the places where they are sold.
- Where are some of the foods you eat grown?
- Can you translate something from English into another language?
- What does the meaning *across* have to do with a transplant?

Do It
Let's play the game Telephone. We'll sit in a circle and send a message from one person to the next. I'll whisper something in my neighbor's ear, then they'll pass it on, until it goes all the way around the circle. Can we transmit the message accurately?

©Primary Concepts

unicorn uni (one)

Word Story

One of the Wordly girls is obsessed with unicorns. She loves horses, which led to her interest in unicorns. At first she thought that unicorns had really existed at some time in history, but now she understands that the one-horned creatures are make-believe.

A *unicorn* is a make-believe creature that looks like a horse with a single horn in the middle of its forehead.

In Other Words

unicycle　　　uniform　　　unique　　　unison

Talk About It

- ✪ Have you ever seen anyone ride a unicycle? What do you think the trick is?
- ✪ What types of uniforms have you worn?
- ✪ How are you unique — different from others you know?

Do It

Let's say the alphabet in unison so we sound like one single voice. Try to keep pace with me.

©Primary Concepts

Index

Here you can find word parts listed alphabetically.

able	10	in	21	port	50
aqua	4	inter	44	post	31
astro	36	ir	45	pre	32
aud	37	less	6	ques	51
auto	19	mag	26	scope	42
bi	23	mar	46	self	13
bio	38	mem	27	struct	33
cap	3	micro	47	sub	34
cent	24	mid	8	super	52
con	20	mil	28	tele	53
contra	41	mini	2	terr	54
cycle	43	mis	9	therm	40
dis	25	multi	48	trans	55
du	5	non	29	tri	35
ex	17	oct	11	un	22
flex	39	over	30	under	15
ful	1	ped	12	uni	56
ician	14	phone	49	vis	18
im	7	pop	16		

©Primary Concepts

58

Index

Here the focus words for each lesson are listed alphabetically.

aquarium 4	inhale 21	postpone 31
astronomy 36	interrupt 44	preview 32
audio 37	irreparable 45	request 51
automatic 19	magnificent 26	selfish 13
bilingual 23	marina 46	stethoscope 42
biography 38	memorable 27	subway 34
captain 3	microscope 47	supervise 52
careless 6	midnight 8	symphony 49
century 24	millionaire 28	telescope 53
cheerful 1	miniature 2	territory 54
conference 20	misunderstand 9	thermostat 40
construction 33	multicolored 48	transfer 55
contrary 41	musician 14	tripod 35
cyclone 43	nonstop 29	unable 22
dishonesty 25	octopus 11	undercover 15
duet 5	overdue 30	unicorn 56
exterior 17	pedestrian 12	vision 18
flexible 39	population 16	washable 10
impossible 7	portable 50	

©Primary Concepts